How Does It Grow?

HOW DO PINE TREES GROW?

By Kathleen Connors

Gareth Stevens
PUBLISHING

Please visit our website, www.garethstevens.com. For a free color catalog of all our high-quality books, call toll free 1-800-542-2595 or fax 1-877-542-2596.

Library of Congress Cataloging-in-Publication Data
Names: Connors, Kathleen, author.
Title: How do pine trees grow? / Kathleen Connors.
Description: New York : Gareth Stevens Publishing, [2022] | Series: How does it grow? | Includes index.
Identifiers: LCCN 2020011766 | ISBN 9781538263051 (paperback) | ISBN 9781538263075 (library binding) | ISBN 9781538263068 (6 Pack) | ISBN 9781538263082 (ebook)
Subjects: LCSH: Pine–Juvenile literature.
Classification: LCC SD397.P55 C66 2022 | DDC 585/.2–dc23
LC record available at https://lccn.loc.gov/2020011766

First Edition

Published in 2022 by
Gareth Stevens Publishing
111 East 14th Street, Suite 349
New York, NY 10003

Editor: Kristen Nelson
Designer: Katelyn E. Reynolds

Photo credits: Cover, p. 1 Serg64/Shutterstock.com; p. 5 Misha Kaminsky/E+/Getty Images; p. 7 J-P Lahall / Photolibrary Getty Images Plus; pp. 9, 24 (cone) Karin Sigwarth/ Getty Images; p. 11 Thang Tat Nguyen/ Moment / Getty Images; p. 13 Bob Wickham / Photolibrary / Getty Images Plus; p. 15 Terry W. Eggers /The Image Bank / Getty Images; pp. 17, 24 (trunk) Mark Hamblin/ Oxford Scientific/ Getty Images Plus; pp. 19, 24 (needles) Anne Hyde/ Photolibrary / Getty Images Plus; p. 21 Shehryar Khan/ iStock /Getty Images Plus; p. 23 Michele D'Amico supersky77 /Moment/ Getty Images.

Printed in the United States of America

Contents

Pine trees are found all over.
How do they grow?

They start as seeds.

Seeds are in cones.

Seeds grow in soil.
They need water and sun.

They grow best near the top of the soil.

It takes a long time for seeds to grow.

They grow roots.
The stem is the trunk.

Pine trees have
thin leaves.
These are needles.

The trees grow slowly.
They can be tall!

Sugar pines are
the tallest.

Words to Know

cone

needles

trunk

Index